50 Japanese Food Recipes for Home

By: Kelly Johnson

Table of Contents

- Acai Berry Blast
- Green Goddess Detox
- Tropical Mango Tango
- Berry Banana Bliss
- Spirulina Sunshine
- Pomegranate Powerhouse
- Chocolate Peanut Butter Protein
- Blueberry Burst
- Kale and Kiwi Kickstart
- Antioxidant Avocado
- Dragonfruit Delight
- Raspberry Revival
- Mango Coconut Dream
- Spinach Pineapple Paradise
- Turmeric Tonic
- Super Green Spirulina
- Chia Seed Cherry
- Strawberry Spinach Surprise
- Pineapple Passion
- Banana Almond Energizer
- Golden Glow Mango Turmeric
- Matcha Madness
- Superfood Berry Blast
- Almond Butter Banana
- Kale and Peach Perfection
- Chocolate Cherry Chia
- Acai Blueberry Bliss
- Kiwi Kale Kick
- Mango Turmeric Tango
- Berry Beet Beauty
- Peanut Butter Power
- Pineapple Kale Cooler
- Coconut Berry Burst
- Green Tea Zen
- Dragonfruit Dragonfire

- Berry Blastoff
- Almond Joy Delight
- Mango Ginger Zing
- Super Berry Spinach
- Cocoa Coconut Crush
- Turmeric Mango Magic
- Avocado Almond Dream
- Blueberry Basil Bliss
- Raspberry Coconut Refresher
- Papaya Paradise
- Matcha Mint Marvel
- Chocolate Cherry Bomb
- Green Goodness Galore
- Goldenberry Glow
- Peachy Protein Powerhouse

Acai Berry Blast

Ingredients:

- 1 packet of frozen acai berry puree (unsweetened)
- 1/2 cup of frozen mixed berries (such as strawberries, blueberries, and raspberries)
- 1/2 frozen banana
- 1/2 cup of plain Greek yogurt or almond milk
- 1 tablespoon of honey or agave syrup (optional, adjust to taste)
- 1/2 cup of ice cubes (optional, for a thicker consistency)

Instructions:

1. Remove the frozen acai berry packet from the freezer and run it under warm water for a few seconds to soften slightly.
2. Break the acai berry packet into chunks and place them in a blender.
3. Add the frozen mixed berries, frozen banana, Greek yogurt or almond milk, and honey or agave syrup to the blender.
4. If desired, add ice cubes for a thicker consistency.
5. Blend all the ingredients together until smooth and creamy. If the mixture is too thick, you can add a splash more almond milk to help it blend.
6. Taste the smoothie and adjust sweetness if needed by adding more honey or agave syrup.
7. Once blended to your liking, pour the Acai Berry Blast smoothie into glasses and enjoy immediately!

Feel free to customize this recipe by adding other ingredients like spinach for extra nutrition or protein powder for an added protein boost. Enjoy your Acai Berry Blast!

Green Goddess Detox

Ingredients:

- 1 cup of fresh spinach leaves
- 1/2 cup of chopped kale leaves (stems removed)
- 1/2 cucumber, peeled and chopped
- 1 green apple, cored and chopped
- 1/2 lemon, juiced
- 1-inch piece of fresh ginger, peeled and grated
- 1/2 cup of coconut water or filtered water
- Optional: a few sprigs of fresh mint leaves for extra freshness

Instructions:

1. Wash all the greens thoroughly.
2. Place the spinach, kale, cucumber, green apple, lemon juice, grated ginger, and optional mint leaves into a blender.
3. Add coconut water or filtered water to the blender.
4. Blend all the ingredients until smooth and creamy. If the mixture is too thick, you can add more water to achieve your desired consistency.
5. Taste the smoothie and adjust the flavor by adding more lemon juice if desired.
6. Pour the Green Goddess Detox smoothie into glasses and serve immediately.

This smoothie is packed with vitamins, minerals, and antioxidants from the leafy greens, cucumber, apple, lemon, and ginger. It's hydrating, refreshing, and perfect for a detox or a boost of energy. Enjoy your Green Goddess Detox!

Berry Banana Bliss

Ingredients:

- 1 ripe banana
- 1/2 cup of mixed berries (such as strawberries, blueberries, raspberries)
- 1/2 cup of plain Greek yogurt or almond milk
- 1 tablespoon of honey or maple syrup (optional, adjust to taste)
- 1/2 cup of ice cubes (optional, for a thicker consistency)

Instructions:

1. Peel the ripe banana and break it into chunks.
2. Wash the mixed berries if fresh, or use frozen berries if preferred.
3. Place the banana chunks and mixed berries into a blender.
4. Add the plain Greek yogurt or almond milk to the blender.
5. If desired, add honey or maple syrup for sweetness.
6. Optionally, add ice cubes for a thicker texture.
7. Blend all the ingredients until smooth and creamy. If the mixture is too thick, you can add a splash more almond milk to help it blend.
8. Taste the smoothie and adjust sweetness if needed by adding more honey or maple syrup.
9. Once blended to your liking, pour the Berry Banana Bliss smoothie into glasses and enjoy immediately!

This smoothie is not only delicious but also packed with nutrients from the bananas and mixed berries, while the Greek yogurt adds creaminess and a dose of protein. It's a perfect pick-me-up for any time of the day!

Spirulina Sunshine

Ingredients:

- 1 ripe banana
- 1 cup of pineapple chunks (fresh or frozen)
- 1 cup of spinach leaves
- 1 teaspoon of spirulina powder
- 1/2 cup of coconut water or almond milk
- Optional: 1 tablespoon of honey or maple syrup for added sweetness

Instructions:

1. Peel the ripe banana and break it into chunks.
2. If using fresh pineapple, peel and cut it into chunks. If using frozen pineapple, no need to prep.
3. Wash the spinach leaves thoroughly.
4. Place the banana chunks, pineapple chunks, spinach leaves, spirulina powder, and optional sweetener into a blender.
5. Add coconut water or almond milk to the blender.
6. Blend all the ingredients until smooth and creamy. If the mixture is too thick, you can add more coconut water or almond milk to achieve your desired consistency.
7. Taste the smoothie and adjust sweetness if needed by adding more honey or maple syrup.
8. Once blended to your liking, pour the Spirulina Sunshine smoothie into glasses and serve immediately.

This smoothie is not only visually appealing but also packed with nutrients. Spirulina is a nutrient-rich blue-green algae that is high in protein, vitamins, and minerals, while pineapple provides natural sweetness and vitamin C, and spinach adds additional vitamins and minerals. Enjoy your Spirulina Sunshine smoothie for a refreshing and nutritious treat!

Pomegranate Powerhouse

Ingredients:

- 1 cup of pomegranate seeds (fresh or frozen)
- 1 ripe banana
- 1/2 cup of plain Greek yogurt or coconut yogurt
- 1/2 cup of spinach leaves
- 1 tablespoon of chia seeds
- 1/2 cup of coconut water or almond milk
- Optional: 1 tablespoon of honey or maple syrup for added sweetness

Instructions:

1. If using fresh pomegranate seeds, carefully remove the seeds from the pomegranate. If using frozen seeds, thaw them slightly.
2. Peel the ripe banana and break it into chunks.
3. Wash the spinach leaves thoroughly.
4. Place the pomegranate seeds, banana chunks, spinach leaves, chia seeds, and optional sweetener into a blender.
5. Add Greek yogurt or coconut yogurt and coconut water or almond milk to the blender.
6. Blend all the ingredients until smooth and creamy. If the mixture is too thick, you can add more coconut water or almond milk to reach your desired consistency.
7. Taste the smoothie and adjust sweetness if needed by adding more honey or maple syrup.
8. Once blended to your liking, pour the Pomegranate Powerhouse smoothie into glasses and serve immediately.

This smoothie is packed with antioxidants from the pomegranate seeds, vitamins and minerals from the banana and spinach, and omega-3 fatty acids from the chia seeds. It's a delicious and nutritious way to start your day or refuel after a workout!

Chocolate Peanut Butter Protein

Ingredients:

- 1 ripe banana
- 1 tablespoon of cocoa powder (unsweetened)
- 2 tablespoons of peanut butter (unsweetened)
- 1 scoop of chocolate protein powder
- 1 cup of milk (dairy or plant-based)
- 1/2 cup of Greek yogurt or silken tofu (for extra creaminess and protein)
- Optional: 1 tablespoon of honey or maple syrup (for added sweetness)

Instructions:

1. Peel the ripe banana and break it into chunks.
2. In a blender, combine the banana chunks, cocoa powder, peanut butter, chocolate protein powder, milk, and Greek yogurt or silken tofu.
3. If you prefer a sweeter taste, add honey or maple syrup to the blender.
4. Blend all the ingredients until smooth and creamy. If the mixture is too thick, you can add more milk to achieve your desired consistency.
5. Taste the smoothie and adjust sweetness if needed by adding more honey or maple syrup.
6. Once blended to your liking, pour the Chocolate Peanut Butter Protein smoothie into glasses and serve immediately.

This smoothie is not only indulgent but also packed with protein from the peanut butter, chocolate protein powder, and Greek yogurt or tofu. It's perfect for a post-workout snack or a quick and nutritious breakfast on the go!

Blueberry Burst

Ingredients:

- 1 cup of frozen blueberries
- 1 ripe banana
- 1/2 cup of plain Greek yogurt or coconut yogurt
- 1/2 cup of spinach leaves
- 1 tablespoon of chia seeds
- 1/2 cup of coconut water or almond milk
- Optional: 1 tablespoon of honey or maple syrup for added sweetness

Instructions:

1. Peel the ripe banana and break it into chunks.
2. Wash the spinach leaves thoroughly.
3. In a blender, combine the frozen blueberries, banana chunks, spinach leaves, chia seeds, Greek yogurt or coconut yogurt, and coconut water or almond milk.
4. If you prefer a sweeter taste, add honey or maple syrup to the blender.
5. Blend all the ingredients until smooth and creamy. If the mixture is too thick, you can add more coconut water or almond milk to achieve your desired consistency.
6. Taste the smoothie and adjust sweetness if needed by adding more honey or maple syrup.
7. Once blended to your liking, pour the Blueberry Burst smoothie into glasses and serve immediately.

This smoothie is loaded with antioxidants from the blueberries, vitamins and minerals from the banana and spinach, and omega-3 fatty acids from the chia seeds. It's a delicious and nutritious way to start your day or enjoy as a midday snack!

Kale and Kiwi Kickstart

Ingredients:

- 1 ripe kiwi, peeled and chopped
- 1/2 cup of chopped kale leaves (stems removed)
- 1 ripe banana
- 1/2 cup of pineapple chunks (fresh or frozen)
- 1/2 cup of coconut water or almond milk
- Optional: 1 tablespoon of honey or maple syrup for added sweetness

Instructions:

1. Peel the ripe kiwi and chop it into chunks.
2. Wash the kale leaves thoroughly and remove the stems.
3. Peel the ripe banana and break it into chunks.
4. In a blender, combine the kiwi chunks, chopped kale leaves, banana chunks, pineapple chunks, and coconut water or almond milk.
5. If you prefer a sweeter taste, add honey or maple syrup to the blender.
6. Blend all the ingredients until smooth and creamy. If the mixture is too thick, you can add more coconut water or almond milk to achieve your desired consistency.
7. Taste the smoothie and adjust sweetness if needed by adding more honey or maple syrup.
8. Once blended to your liking, pour the Kale and Kiwi Kickstart smoothie into glasses and serve immediately.

This smoothie is packed with vitamin C from the kiwi and pineapple, nutrients from the kale, and hydration from the coconut water or almond milk. It's a delicious and nutritious way to kickstart your day!

Antioxidant Avocado

Ingredients:

- 1 ripe avocado, peeled and pitted
- 1 cup of mixed berries (such as strawberries, blueberries, and raspberries)
- 1 handful of spinach leaves
- 1 tablespoon of chia seeds
- 1 cup of coconut water or almond milk
- Optional: 1 tablespoon of honey or maple syrup for added sweetness

Instructions:

1. Scoop the flesh of the ripe avocado into a blender.
2. Wash the mixed berries if fresh, or use frozen berries if preferred.
3. Wash the spinach leaves thoroughly.
4. Add the mixed berries, spinach leaves, chia seeds, and coconut water or almond milk to the blender.
5. If you prefer a sweeter taste, add honey or maple syrup to the blender.
6. Blend all the ingredients until smooth and creamy. If the mixture is too thick, you can add more coconut water or almond milk to achieve your desired consistency.
7. Taste the smoothie and adjust sweetness if needed by adding more honey or maple syrup.
8. Once blended to your liking, pour the Antioxidant Avocado smoothie into glasses and serve immediately.

This smoothie is loaded with antioxidants from the berries, healthy fats from the avocado, and nutrients from the spinach and chia seeds. It's a delicious and nutritious way to boost your antioxidant intake and start your day on a healthy note!

Dragonfruit Delight

Ingredients:

- 1 ripe dragon fruit, peeled and chopped
- 1/2 cup of chopped pineapple (fresh or frozen)
- 1/2 cup of chopped mango (fresh or frozen)
- 1/2 cup of coconut water or pineapple juice
- 1 tablespoon of lime juice
- Optional: 1 tablespoon of honey or agave syrup for added sweetness

Instructions:

1. Peel the ripe dragon fruit and chop it into chunks.
2. If using fresh pineapple and mango, peel and chop them into chunks. If using frozen fruit, no need to prep.
3. In a blender, combine the dragon fruit chunks, pineapple chunks, mango chunks, coconut water or pineapple juice, and lime juice.
4. If you prefer a sweeter taste, add honey or agave syrup to the blender.
5. Blend all the ingredients until smooth and creamy. If the mixture is too thick, you can add more coconut water or pineapple juice to achieve your desired consistency.
6. Taste the smoothie and adjust sweetness if needed by adding more honey or agave syrup.
7. Once blended to your liking, pour the Dragonfruit Delight smoothie into glasses and serve immediately.

This smoothie is not only visually stunning but also packed with tropical flavors and nutrients. Dragon fruit is rich in antioxidants and vitamin C, while pineapple and mango add natural sweetness and additional vitamins. It's a delightful and refreshing treat!

Raspberry Revival

Ingredients:

- 1 cup of fresh or frozen raspberries
- 1 ripe banana
- 1/2 cup of plain Greek yogurt or coconut yogurt
- 1/2 cup of spinach leaves
- 1 tablespoon of chia seeds
- 1/2 cup of coconut water or almond milk
- Optional: 1 tablespoon of honey or maple syrup for added sweetness

Instructions:

1. Wash the raspberries thoroughly if using fresh ones.
2. Peel the ripe banana and break it into chunks.
3. Wash the spinach leaves thoroughly.
4. In a blender, combine the raspberries, banana chunks, Greek yogurt or coconut yogurt, spinach leaves, chia seeds, and coconut water or almond milk.
5. If you prefer a sweeter taste, add honey or maple syrup to the blender.
6. Blend all the ingredients until smooth and creamy. If the mixture is too thick, you can add more coconut water or almond milk to achieve your desired consistency.
7. Taste the smoothie and adjust sweetness if needed by adding more honey or maple syrup.
8. Once blended to your liking, pour the Raspberry Revival smoothie into glasses and serve immediately.

This smoothie is bursting with the tangy sweetness of raspberries, along with the creaminess of banana and yogurt. The addition of spinach adds extra nutrients, while chia seeds provide fiber and omega-3 fatty acids. It's a perfect way to revive your energy levels and start your day on a refreshing note!

Mango Coconut Dream

Ingredients:

- 1 ripe mango, peeled and chopped
- 1/2 cup of chopped pineapple (fresh or frozen)
- 1/2 cup of coconut milk
- 1/2 cup of coconut water
- 1 tablespoon of lime juice
- Optional: 1 tablespoon of honey or agave syrup for added sweetness

Instructions:

1. Peel the ripe mango and chop it into chunks.
2. If using fresh pineapple, peel and chop it into chunks. If using frozen pineapple, no need to prep.
3. In a blender, combine the mango chunks, pineapple chunks, coconut milk, coconut water, and lime juice.
4. If you prefer a sweeter taste, add honey or agave syrup to the blender.
5. Blend all the ingredients until smooth and creamy. If the mixture is too thick, you can add more coconut water to achieve your desired consistency.
6. Taste the smoothie and adjust sweetness if needed by adding more honey or agave syrup.
7. Once blended to your liking, pour the Mango Coconut Dream smoothie into glasses and serve immediately.

This smoothie is a tropical paradise in a glass! The creamy coconut milk and refreshing coconut water complement the sweetness of mango and pineapple perfectly. The hint of lime adds a zesty twist. It's a dreamy and indulgent treat that will transport you to the tropics with every sip!

Spinach Pineapple Paradise

Ingredients:

- 1 cup of fresh spinach leaves
- 1 cup of chopped pineapple (fresh or frozen)
- 1 ripe banana
- 1/2 cup of coconut water or almond milk
- 1 tablespoon of chia seeds
- Optional: 1 tablespoon of honey or maple syrup for added sweetness

Instructions:

1. Wash the spinach leaves thoroughly.
2. If using fresh pineapple, peel and chop it into chunks. If using frozen pineapple, no need to prep.
3. Peel the ripe banana and break it into chunks.
4. In a blender, combine the spinach leaves, pineapple chunks, banana chunks, coconut water or almond milk, and chia seeds.
5. If you prefer a sweeter taste, add honey or maple syrup to the blender.
6. Blend all the ingredients until smooth and creamy. If the mixture is too thick, you can add more coconut water or almond milk to achieve your desired consistency.
7. Taste the smoothie and adjust sweetness if needed by adding more honey or maple syrup.
8. Once blended to your liking, pour the Spinach Pineapple Paradise smoothie into glasses and serve immediately.

This smoothie is packed with vitamins, minerals, and antioxidants from the spinach and pineapple. The banana adds creaminess, while the chia seeds provide fiber and omega-3 fatty acids. It's a refreshing and nutritious way to start your day or enjoy as a midday snack!

Turmeric Tonic

Ingredients:

- 1 teaspoon of ground turmeric or 1-inch piece of fresh turmeric root, peeled and grated
- 1/2 teaspoon of ground ginger or 1-inch piece of fresh ginger root, peeled and grated
- 1/2 teaspoon of ground cinnamon
- Pinch of ground black pepper (helps with turmeric absorption)
- 1 tablespoon of honey or maple syrup (adjust to taste)
- Juice of 1/2 lemon
- 2 cups of warm water
- Optional: a dash of cayenne pepper for added heat

Instructions:

1. In a mug or glass, combine the ground turmeric, ground ginger, ground cinnamon, ground black pepper, and honey or maple syrup.
2. Squeeze in the juice of half a lemon.
3. Pour in the warm water and stir until all the ingredients are well combined.
4. Taste the turmeric tonic and adjust sweetness or spice level if needed.
5. Optionally, sprinkle a dash of cayenne pepper on top for added heat.
6. Enjoy your Turmeric Tonic while warm.

This tonic is not only delicious but also potentially offers various health benefits attributed to the anti-inflammatory properties of turmeric and ginger. It's a soothing and invigorating beverage that's perfect for any time of the day, especially during colder weather or when you need a little pick-me-up!

Super Green Spirulina

Ingredients:

- 1 ripe banana
- 1/2 cup of pineapple chunks (fresh or frozen)
- 1/2 cup of mango chunks (fresh or frozen)
- 1 handful of spinach leaves
- 1 teaspoon of spirulina powder
- 1/2 cup of coconut water or almond milk
- Optional: 1 tablespoon of honey or maple syrup for added sweetness

Instructions:

1. Peel the ripe banana and break it into chunks.
2. If using fresh pineapple and mango, peel and chop them into chunks. If using frozen fruit, no need to prep.
3. Wash the spinach leaves thoroughly.
4. In a blender, combine the banana chunks, pineapple chunks, mango chunks, spinach leaves, spirulina powder, and coconut water or almond milk.
5. If you prefer a sweeter taste, add honey or maple syrup to the blender.
6. Blend all the ingredients until smooth and creamy. If the mixture is too thick, you can add more coconut water or almond milk to achieve your desired consistency.
7. Taste the smoothie and adjust sweetness if needed by adding more honey or maple syrup.
8. Once blended to your liking, pour the Super Green Spirulina smoothie into glasses and serve immediately.

This smoothie is packed with nutrients from the fruits and vegetables, while spirulina adds an extra boost of protein, vitamins, and minerals. It's a refreshing and energizing way to start your day or enjoy as a post-workout snack!

Chia Seed Cherry

Ingredients:

- 1 cup of pitted cherries (fresh or frozen)
- 1 tablespoon of chia seeds
- 1/2 cup of Greek yogurt or coconut yogurt
- 1/2 cup of almond milk or any milk of your choice
- Optional: 1 tablespoon of honey or maple syrup for added sweetness

Instructions:

1. If using fresh cherries, pit them. If using frozen cherries, no need to pit.
2. In a blender, combine the pitted cherries, chia seeds, Greek yogurt or coconut yogurt, almond milk, and optional honey or maple syrup.
3. Blend all the ingredients until smooth and creamy. If the mixture is too thick, you can add more almond milk to achieve your desired consistency.
4. Taste the smoothie and adjust sweetness if needed by adding more honey or maple syrup.
5. Once blended to your liking, pour the Chia Seed Cherry smoothie into glasses and serve immediately.

This smoothie is rich in antioxidants from the cherries and omega-3 fatty acids from the chia seeds. The yogurt adds creaminess and a boost of protein, while almond milk provides a dairy-free base. It's a satisfying and refreshing drink that's perfect for any time of the day!

Strawberry Spinach Surprise

Ingredients:

- 1 cup of fresh spinach leaves
- 1 cup of frozen strawberries
- 1 ripe banana
- 1/2 cup of Greek yogurt or coconut yogurt
- 1/2 cup of almond milk or any milk of your choice
- Optional: 1 tablespoon of honey or maple syrup for added sweetness

Instructions:

1. Wash the spinach leaves thoroughly.
2. Peel the ripe banana and break it into chunks.
3. In a blender, combine the spinach leaves, frozen strawberries, banana chunks, Greek yogurt or coconut yogurt, and almond milk.
4. If you prefer a sweeter taste, add honey or maple syrup to the blender.
5. Blend all the ingredients until smooth and creamy. If the mixture is too thick, you can add more almond milk to achieve your desired consistency.
6. Taste the smoothie and adjust sweetness if needed by adding more honey or maple syrup.
7. Once blended to your liking, pour the Strawberry Spinach Surprise smoothie into glasses and serve immediately.

This smoothie is packed with vitamins, minerals, and antioxidants from the spinach and strawberries. The banana adds creaminess and natural sweetness, while the yogurt provides probiotics and protein. It's a delicious and nutritious way to sneak some greens into your diet and enjoy a refreshing treat!

Pineapple Passion

Ingredients:

- 1 cup of chopped pineapple (fresh or frozen)
- 1 ripe banana
- 1/2 cup of Greek yogurt or coconut yogurt
- 1/2 cup of coconut water or pineapple juice
- Optional: 1 tablespoon of honey or maple syrup for added sweetness
- Ice cubes (if not using frozen pineapple)

Instructions:

1. If using fresh pineapple, peel and chop it into chunks.
2. Peel the ripe banana and break it into chunks.
3. In a blender, combine the chopped pineapple, banana chunks, Greek yogurt or coconut yogurt, and coconut water or pineapple juice.
4. If you prefer a sweeter taste, add honey or maple syrup to the blender.
5. If you're not using frozen pineapple and want a colder smoothie, add a handful of ice cubes.
6. Blend all the ingredients until smooth and creamy. If the mixture is too thick, you can add more coconut water or pineapple juice to achieve your desired consistency.
7. Taste the smoothie and adjust sweetness if needed by adding more honey or maple syrup.
8. Once blended to your liking, pour the Pineapple Passion smoothie into glasses and serve immediately.

This smoothie is bursting with the tropical flavors of pineapple and coconut. It's refreshing, creamy, and perfect for enjoying on a warm day or as a quick breakfast or snack any time of the year!

Banana Almond Energizer

Ingredients:

- 1 ripe banana
- 1 tablespoon of almond butter
- 1 tablespoon of chia seeds
- 1/2 cup of almond milk or any milk of your choice
- 1/2 cup of Greek yogurt or coconut yogurt
- Optional: 1 teaspoon of honey or maple syrup for added sweetness
- Ice cubes (optional, for a colder smoothie)

Instructions:

1. Peel the ripe banana and break it into chunks.
2. In a blender, combine the banana chunks, almond butter, chia seeds, almond milk, and Greek yogurt.
3. If you prefer a sweeter taste, add honey or maple syrup to the blender.
4. Optionally, add a few ice cubes if you want a colder smoothie.
5. Blend all the ingredients until smooth and creamy. If the mixture is too thick, you can add more almond milk to achieve your desired consistency.
6. Taste the smoothie and adjust sweetness if needed by adding more honey or maple syrup.
7. Once blended to your liking, pour the Banana Almond Energizer smoothie into glasses and serve immediately.

This smoothie is a great source of energy, thanks to the natural sugars in the banana and the healthy fats and protein in the almond butter and Greek yogurt. The chia seeds also provide an extra boost of fiber and omega-3 fatty acids. It's a delicious and satisfying way to start your day or refuel after a workout!

Golden Glow Mango Turmeric

Ingredients:

- 1 cup of chopped mango (fresh or frozen)
- 1 ripe banana
- 1 teaspoon of ground turmeric or 1-inch piece of fresh turmeric root, peeled and grated
- 1/2 teaspoon of ground ginger or 1-inch piece of fresh ginger root, peeled and grated
- 1/2 cup of Greek yogurt or coconut yogurt
- 1/2 cup of almond milk or any milk of your choice
- Optional: 1 tablespoon of honey or maple syrup for added sweetness
- Ice cubes (optional, for a colder smoothie)

Instructions:

1. If using fresh mango, peel and chop it into chunks. If using frozen mango, no need to prep.
2. Peel the ripe banana and break it into chunks.
3. In a blender, combine the chopped mango, banana chunks, ground turmeric or grated fresh turmeric, ground ginger or grated fresh ginger, Greek yogurt, and almond milk.
4. If you prefer a sweeter taste, add honey or maple syrup to the blender.
5. Optionally, add a few ice cubes if you want a colder smoothie.
6. Blend all the ingredients until smooth and creamy. If the mixture is too thick, you can add more almond milk to achieve your desired consistency.
7. Taste the smoothie and adjust sweetness if needed by adding more honey or maple syrup.
8. Once blended to your liking, pour the Golden Glow Mango Turmeric smoothie into glasses and serve immediately.

This smoothie combines the tropical sweetness of mango with the anti-inflammatory properties of turmeric and ginger, creating a delicious and healthful drink. It's perfect for boosting your immune system and providing a refreshing pick-me-up!

Matcha Madness

Ingredients:

- 1 teaspoon of matcha powder
- 1 cup of unsweetened almond milk or any milk of your choice
- 1 ripe banana
- 1 tablespoon of honey or maple syrup (optional, for added sweetness)
- Ice cubes (optional, for a colder smoothie)

Instructions:

1. In a blender, combine the matcha powder and almond milk.
2. Add the ripe banana to the blender.
3. If you prefer a sweeter taste, add honey or maple syrup to the blender.
4. Optionally, add a few ice cubes if you want a colder smoothie.
5. Blend all the ingredients until smooth and creamy. If the mixture is too thick, you can add more almond milk to achieve your desired consistency.
6. Taste the smoothie and adjust sweetness if needed by adding more honey or maple syrup.
7. Once blended to your liking, pour the Matcha Madness smoothie into glasses and serve immediately.

This smoothie is not only delicious but also packed with antioxidants and nutrients from the matcha powder and banana. It's a great way to boost your energy levels and focus, making it perfect for a morning pick-me-up or a midday refreshment!

Superfood Berry Blast

Ingredients:

- 1 cup of mixed berries (such as strawberries, blueberries, raspberries)
- 1 ripe banana
- 1 tablespoon of chia seeds
- 1 tablespoon of flaxseed meal
- 1 tablespoon of hemp seeds
- 1 cup of spinach leaves
- 1/2 cup of Greek yogurt or coconut yogurt
- 1/2 cup of almond milk or any milk of your choice
- Optional: 1 tablespoon of honey or maple syrup for added sweetness
- Ice cubes (optional, for a colder smoothie)

Instructions:

1. Wash the mixed berries thoroughly if using fresh ones.
2. Peel the ripe banana and break it into chunks.
3. In a blender, combine the mixed berries, banana chunks, chia seeds, flaxseed meal, hemp seeds, spinach leaves, Greek yogurt, and almond milk.
4. If you prefer a sweeter taste, add honey or maple syrup to the blender.
5. Optionally, add a few ice cubes if you want a colder smoothie.
6. Blend all the ingredients until smooth and creamy. If the mixture is too thick, you can add more almond milk to achieve your desired consistency.
7. Taste the smoothie and adjust sweetness if needed by adding more honey or maple syrup.
8. Once blended to your liking, pour the Superfood Berry Blast smoothie into glasses and serve immediately.

This smoothie is packed with antioxidants, fiber, omega-3 fatty acids, and essential nutrients from the berries, seeds, spinach, and yogurt. It's a delicious and satisfying way to start your day or enjoy as a post-workout snack!

Almond Butter Banana

Ingredients:

- 1 ripe banana
- 1 tablespoon of almond butter
- 1 cup of almond milk or any milk of your choice
- Optional: 1 tablespoon of honey or maple syrup for added sweetness
- Ice cubes (optional, for a colder smoothie)

Instructions:

1. Peel the ripe banana and break it into chunks.
2. In a blender, combine the banana chunks, almond butter, and almond milk.
3. If you prefer a sweeter taste, add honey or maple syrup to the blender.
4. Optionally, add a few ice cubes if you want a colder smoothie.
5. Blend all the ingredients until smooth and creamy. If the mixture is too thick, you can add more almond milk to achieve your desired consistency.
6. Taste the smoothie and adjust sweetness if needed by adding more honey or maple syrup.
7. Once blended to your liking, pour the Almond Butter Banana smoothie into glasses and serve immediately.

This smoothie is rich in potassium, healthy fats, and protein from the banana and almond butter. It's a great way to start your day or enjoy as a quick and nutritious snack!

Kale and Peach Perfection

Ingredients:

- 1 cup of chopped kale leaves (stems removed)
- 1 ripe peach, pitted and chopped
- 1 ripe banana
- 1/2 cup of Greek yogurt or coconut yogurt
- 1/2 cup of almond milk or any milk of your choice
- Optional: 1 tablespoon of honey or maple syrup for added sweetness
- Ice cubes (optional, for a colder smoothie)

Instructions:

1. Wash the kale leaves thoroughly and remove the stems.
2. Pit and chop the ripe peach.
3. Peel the ripe banana and break it into chunks.
4. In a blender, combine the chopped kale leaves, chopped peach, banana chunks, Greek yogurt, and almond milk.
5. If you prefer a sweeter taste, add honey or maple syrup to the blender.
6. Optionally, add a few ice cubes if you want a colder smoothie.
7. Blend all the ingredients until smooth and creamy. If the mixture is too thick, you can add more almond milk to achieve your desired consistency.
8. Taste the smoothie and adjust sweetness if needed by adding more honey or maple syrup.
9. Once blended to your liking, pour the Kale and Peach Perfection smoothie into glasses and serve immediately.

This smoothie combines the sweetness of peaches with the nutritional powerhouse of kale, creating a delicious and refreshing drink. It's packed with vitamins, minerals, and antioxidants, making it a perfect choice for a healthy breakfast or snack!

Chocolate Cherry Chia

Ingredients:

- 1 cup of pitted cherries (fresh or frozen)
- 1 tablespoon of cocoa powder (unsweetened)
- 1 tablespoon of chia seeds
- 1/2 cup of Greek yogurt or coconut yogurt
- 1/2 cup of almond milk or any milk of your choice
- Optional: 1 tablespoon of honey or maple syrup for added sweetness
- Ice cubes (optional, for a colder smoothie)

Instructions:

1. If using fresh cherries, pit them. If using frozen cherries, no need to pit.
2. In a blender, combine the pitted cherries, cocoa powder, chia seeds, Greek yogurt, and almond milk.
3. If you prefer a sweeter taste, add honey or maple syrup to the blender.
4. Optionally, add a few ice cubes if you want a colder smoothie.
5. Blend all the ingredients until smooth and creamy. If the mixture is too thick, you can add more almond milk to achieve your desired consistency.
6. Taste the smoothie and adjust sweetness if needed by adding more honey or maple syrup.
7. Once blended to your liking, pour the Chocolate Cherry Chia smoothie into glasses and serve immediately.

This smoothie is a delightful combination of rich chocolate flavor from the cocoa powder, tartness from the cherries, and the added texture and nutrition from the chia seeds. It's perfect for satisfying your sweet cravings while providing a boost of energy and essential nutrients!

Acai Blueberry Bliss

Ingredients:

- 1 packet of frozen acai puree (unsweetened)
- 1/2 cup of frozen blueberries
- 1 ripe banana
- 1/2 cup of Greek yogurt or coconut yogurt
- 1/2 cup of almond milk or any milk of your choice
- Optional: 1 tablespoon of honey or maple syrup for added sweetness
- Optional toppings: fresh blueberries, granola, sliced banana, shredded coconut

Instructions:

1. Run the packet of frozen acai puree under warm water for a few seconds to slightly thaw it.
2. Break the thawed acai puree into chunks and add it to a blender.
3. Add the frozen blueberries, ripe banana, Greek yogurt, almond milk, and optional honey or maple syrup to the blender.
4. Blend all the ingredients until smooth and creamy. If the mixture is too thick, you can add more almond milk to achieve your desired consistency.
5. Taste the smoothie and adjust sweetness if needed by adding more honey or maple syrup.
6. Once blended to your liking, pour the Acai Blueberry Bliss smoothie into glasses.
7. Optionally, top the smoothie with fresh blueberries, granola, sliced banana, or shredded coconut for extra flavor and texture.
8. Serve immediately and enjoy your Acai Blueberry Bliss smoothie!

This smoothie is not only delicious but also packed with antioxidants from the acai and blueberries. The banana adds creaminess, while the Greek yogurt provides probiotics and protein. It's a refreshing and nutritious way to start your day or enjoy as a satisfying snack!

Kiwi Kale Kick

Ingredients:

- 1 ripe kiwi, peeled and chopped
- 1 cup of chopped kale leaves (stems removed)
- 1/2 banana
- 1/2 cup of chopped pineapple (fresh or frozen)
- 1/2 cup of coconut water or almond milk
- Optional: 1 tablespoon of honey or maple syrup for added sweetness

Instructions:

1. Peel the ripe kiwi and chop it into chunks.
2. Wash the kale leaves thoroughly and remove the stems.
3. Peel the banana and break it into chunks.
4. In a blender, combine the chopped kiwi, kale leaves, banana chunks, chopped pineapple, and coconut water or almond milk.
5. If you prefer a sweeter taste, add honey or maple syrup to the blender.
6. Blend all the ingredients until smooth and creamy. If the mixture is too thick, you can add more coconut water or almond milk to achieve your desired consistency.
7. Taste the smoothie and adjust sweetness if needed by adding more honey or maple syrup.
8. Once blended to your liking, pour the Kiwi Kale Kick smoothie into glasses and serve immediately.

This smoothie is packed with vitamins, minerals, and antioxidants from the kiwi, kale, banana, and pineapple. It's a refreshing and nutritious way to start your day or enjoy as a midday pick-me-up!

Mango Turmeric Tango

Ingredients:

- 1 cup of chopped mango (fresh or frozen)
- 1 teaspoon of ground turmeric or 1-inch piece of fresh turmeric root, peeled and grated
- 1/2 cup of Greek yogurt or coconut yogurt
- 1/2 cup of almond milk or any milk of your choice
- 1 tablespoon of honey or maple syrup (optional, for added sweetness)
- Optional: a pinch of black pepper (to enhance turmeric absorption)
- Ice cubes (optional, for a colder smoothie)

Instructions:

1. If using fresh mango, peel and chop it into chunks. If using frozen mango, no need to prep.
2. In a blender, combine the chopped mango, ground turmeric or grated fresh turmeric, Greek yogurt, almond milk, and optional honey or maple syrup.
3. Optionally, add a pinch of black pepper to the blender to enhance the absorption of turmeric.
4. If you prefer a colder smoothie, add a few ice cubes to the blender.
5. Blend all the ingredients until smooth and creamy. If the mixture is too thick, you can add more almond milk to achieve your desired consistency.
6. Taste the smoothie and adjust sweetness if needed by adding more honey or maple syrup.
7. Once blended to your liking, pour the Mango Turmeric Tango smoothie into glasses and serve immediately.

This smoothie is bursting with tropical flavor from the mango and offers the potential health benefits of turmeric, such as its anti-inflammatory and antioxidant properties. It's a refreshing and nutritious drink that's perfect for any time of the day!

Berry Beet Beauty

Ingredients:

- 1/2 cup of cooked and cooled beetroot, chopped
- 1/2 cup of mixed berries (such as strawberries, blueberries, raspberries)
- 1 ripe banana
- 1/2 cup of Greek yogurt or coconut yogurt
- 1/2 cup of almond milk or any milk of your choice
- Optional: 1 tablespoon of honey or maple syrup for added sweetness
- Ice cubes (optional, for a colder smoothie)

Instructions:

1. Cook beetroot until tender, then allow it to cool before using it in the smoothie.
2. In a blender, combine the cooked and cooled beetroot, mixed berries, ripe banana, Greek yogurt, and almond milk.
3. If you prefer a sweeter taste, add honey or maple syrup to the blender.
4. Optionally, add a few ice cubes if you want a colder smoothie.
5. Blend all the ingredients until smooth and creamy. If the mixture is too thick, you can add more almond milk to achieve your desired consistency.
6. Taste the smoothie and adjust sweetness if needed by adding more honey or maple syrup.
7. Once blended to your liking, pour the Berry Beet Beauty smoothie into glasses and serve immediately.

This smoothie is packed with antioxidants from the mixed berries and beetroot, providing a burst of color and nutrition. The banana adds creaminess, while the Greek yogurt provides probiotics and protein. It's a refreshing and nutritious way to start your day or enjoy as a midday snack!

Peanut Butter Power

Ingredients:

- 1 ripe banana
- 2 tablespoons of peanut butter
- 1 cup of almond milk or any milk of your choice
- 1/4 cup of rolled oats
- 1 tablespoon of chia seeds
- Optional: 1 tablespoon of honey or maple syrup for added sweetness
- Ice cubes (optional, for a colder smoothie)

Instructions:

1. Peel the ripe banana and break it into chunks.
2. In a blender, combine the banana chunks, peanut butter, almond milk, rolled oats, and chia seeds.
3. If you prefer a sweeter taste, add honey or maple syrup to the blender.
4. Optionally, add a few ice cubes if you want a colder smoothie.
5. Blend all the ingredients until smooth and creamy. If the mixture is too thick, you can add more almond milk to achieve your desired consistency.
6. Taste the smoothie and adjust sweetness if needed by adding more honey or maple syrup.
7. Once blended to your liking, pour the Peanut Butter Power smoothie into glasses and serve immediately.

This smoothie is rich in protein, healthy fats, and fiber from the peanut butter, banana, oats, and chia seeds, providing long-lasting energy and satiety. It's a delicious and nutritious option for breakfast or as a post-workout refuel!

Pineapple Kale Cooler

Ingredients:

- 1 cup of chopped pineapple (fresh or frozen)
- 1 cup of chopped kale leaves (stems removed)
- 1/2 cup of coconut water or pineapple juice
- 1/2 cup of Greek yogurt or coconut yogurt
- Juice of 1/2 lime
- Optional: 1 tablespoon of honey or maple syrup for added sweetness
- Ice cubes (optional, for a colder smoothie)

Instructions:

1. If using fresh pineapple, peel and chop it into chunks. If using frozen pineapple, no need to prep.
2. Wash the kale leaves thoroughly and remove the stems.
3. In a blender, combine the chopped pineapple, chopped kale leaves, coconut water or pineapple juice, Greek yogurt, and lime juice.
4. If you prefer a sweeter taste, add honey or maple syrup to the blender.
5. Optionally, add a few ice cubes if you want a colder smoothie.
6. Blend all the ingredients until smooth and creamy. If the mixture is too thick, you can add more coconut water or pineapple juice to achieve your desired consistency.
7. Taste the smoothie and adjust sweetness if needed by adding more honey or maple syrup.
8. Once blended to your liking, pour the Pineapple Kale Cooler smoothie into glasses and serve immediately.

This smoothie is packed with vitamins, minerals, and antioxidants from the pineapple and kale. The coconut water adds hydration and electrolytes, while the Greek yogurt provides probiotics and protein. It's a refreshing and nutritious drink that's perfect for cooling down on a hot day or enjoying as a post-workout refreshment!

Coconut Berry Burst

Ingredients:

- 1 cup of mixed berries (such as strawberries, blueberries, raspberries)
- 1/2 cup of coconut milk
- 1/2 cup of Greek yogurt or coconut yogurt
- 1 tablespoon of shredded coconut (unsweetened)
- Optional: 1 tablespoon of honey or maple syrup for added sweetness
- Ice cubes (optional, for a colder smoothie)

Instructions:

1. Wash the mixed berries thoroughly if using fresh ones.
2. In a blender, combine the mixed berries, coconut milk, Greek yogurt, and shredded coconut.
3. If you prefer a sweeter taste, add honey or maple syrup to the blender.
4. Optionally, add a few ice cubes if you want a colder smoothie.
5. Blend all the ingredients until smooth and creamy. If the mixture is too thick, you can add more coconut milk to achieve your desired consistency.
6. Taste the smoothie and adjust sweetness if needed by adding more honey or maple syrup.
7. Once blended to your liking, pour the Coconut Berry Burst smoothie into glasses and serve immediately.

This smoothie is bursting with tropical flavor from the coconut milk and shredded coconut, complemented by the sweetness of the mixed berries. It's a delicious and nutritious way to start your day or enjoy as a refreshing snack!

Green Tea Zen

Ingredients:

- 1 green tea bag or 1 teaspoon of loose green tea leaves
- 1 cup of hot water
- 1/2 teaspoon of honey or maple syrup (optional, for added sweetness)
- Juice of 1/2 lemon
- Ice cubes

Instructions:

1. Place the green tea bag or loose green tea leaves in a cup.
2. Pour hot water over the tea bag or leaves.
3. Let the tea steep for about 3-5 minutes, depending on your preference for strength.
4. Once the tea has steeped, remove the tea bag or strain the tea leaves.
5. If you prefer a sweeter taste, stir in honey or maple syrup until dissolved.
6. Squeeze the juice of half a lemon into the tea and stir well.
7. Allow the tea to cool slightly, then transfer it to the refrigerator to chill for about 30 minutes.
8. Once chilled, pour the Green Tea Zen over ice cubes in a glass.
9. Garnish with a lemon slice or mint leaves if desired.
10. Serve and enjoy your Green Tea Zen as a refreshing and calming beverage!

This drink is not only hydrating but also provides the benefits of green tea, known for its antioxidants and potential health-promoting properties. It's perfect for sipping on a hot day or as a soothing beverage to unwind and relax.

Dragonfruit Dragonfire

Ingredients:

- 1 dragon fruit (also known as pitaya), peeled and diced
- 1/2 cup of pineapple chunks (fresh or frozen)
- 1/2 cup of coconut water or coconut milk
- 1 tablespoon of lime juice
- 1/2 teaspoon of cayenne pepper (adjust to taste)
- Optional: 1 tablespoon of honey or agave syrup for added sweetness
- Ice cubes

Instructions:

1. In a blender, combine the diced dragon fruit, pineapple chunks, coconut water or coconut milk, lime juice, and cayenne pepper.
2. If you prefer a sweeter taste, add honey or agave syrup to the blender.
3. Optionally, add a few ice cubes to the blender for a colder drink.
4. Blend all the ingredients until smooth and well combined.
5. Taste the mixture and adjust the sweetness or spiciness according to your preference by adding more honey, agave syrup, or cayenne pepper.
6. Once blended to your liking, pour the Dragonfruit Dragonfire mixture into glasses.
7. Serve immediately and enjoy your fiery and refreshing Dragonfruit Dragonfire drink!

This beverage is not only visually striking but also offers a unique combination of flavors, from the tropical sweetness of dragon fruit and pineapple to the fiery kick of cayenne pepper. It's perfect for adding some excitement to your day or serving as a bold and refreshing party drink! Adjust the spiciness level to your liking for a personalized experience.

Berry Blastoff

Ingredients:

- 1 cup of mixed berries (such as strawberries, blueberries, raspberries)
- 1/2 cup of Greek yogurt or coconut yogurt
- 1/2 cup of orange juice
- 1 tablespoon of honey or maple syrup (optional, for added sweetness)
- Ice cubes (optional)

Instructions:

1. Wash the mixed berries thoroughly if using fresh ones.
2. In a blender, combine the mixed berries, Greek yogurt, orange juice, and optional honey or maple syrup.
3. Optionally, add a few ice cubes to the blender for a colder drink.
4. Blend all the ingredients until smooth and creamy.
5. Taste the mixture and adjust sweetness if needed by adding more honey or maple syrup.
6. Once blended to your liking, pour the Berry Blastoff into glasses.
7. Serve immediately and enjoy your vibrant and delicious Berry Blastoff drink!

This smoothie is bursting with the flavors and nutrients of mixed berries, providing a refreshing and energizing beverage. It's perfect for starting your day on a high note or enjoying as a midday pick-me-up! Adjust the sweetness level according to your taste preferences for a personalized experience.

Almond Joy Delight

Ingredients:

- 1 ripe banana
- 1 cup of almond milk or any milk of your choice
- 2 tablespoons of cocoa powder (unsweetened)
- 1 tablespoon of almond butter
- 1 tablespoon of shredded coconut (unsweetened)
- 1 tablespoon of honey or maple syrup (optional, for added sweetness)
- Ice cubes (optional, for a colder drink)

Instructions:

1. Peel the ripe banana and break it into chunks.
2. In a blender, combine the banana chunks, almond milk, cocoa powder, almond butter, shredded coconut, and optional honey or maple syrup.
3. Optionally, add a few ice cubes to the blender for a colder drink.
4. Blend all the ingredients until smooth and creamy.
5. Taste the mixture and adjust sweetness if needed by adding more honey or maple syrup.
6. Once blended to your liking, pour the Almond Joy Delight into glasses.
7. Optionally, garnish with additional shredded coconut or a sprinkle of cocoa powder.
8. Serve immediately and enjoy your indulgent and satisfying Almond Joy Delight!

This creamy and chocolaty smoothie is reminiscent of the flavors of an Almond Joy candy bar, but with healthier ingredients. It's perfect for satisfying your sweet tooth while providing a boost of energy and nutrients. Feel free to customize the recipe by adding a splash of vanilla extract or a handful of almonds for extra crunch!

Mango Ginger Zing

Ingredients:

- 1 ripe mango, peeled and diced
- 1-inch piece of fresh ginger, peeled and grated
- 1/2 cup of Greek yogurt or coconut yogurt
- 1/2 cup of coconut water or water
- Juice of 1 lime
- Optional: 1 tablespoon of honey or maple syrup for added sweetness
- Ice cubes (optional)

Instructions:

1. Peel and dice the ripe mango.
2. Peel and grate the fresh ginger.
3. In a blender, combine the diced mango, grated ginger, Greek yogurt, coconut water or water, and lime juice.
4. If you prefer a sweeter taste, add honey or maple syrup to the blender.
5. Optionally, add a few ice cubes to the blender for a colder drink.
6. Blend all the ingredients until smooth and creamy.
7. Taste the mixture and adjust sweetness or spiciness if needed by adding more honey, lime juice, or grated ginger.
8. Once blended to your liking, pour the Mango Ginger Zing into glasses.
9. Serve immediately and enjoy your refreshing and zesty Mango Ginger Zing drink!

This smoothie offers the tropical sweetness of mango combined with the spicy kick of fresh ginger, creating a harmonious flavor profile that is both refreshing and invigorating. It's perfect for starting your day on a zesty note or enjoying as a midday pick-me-up! Adjust the sweetness and spiciness levels according to your taste preferences for a personalized experience.

Super Berry Spinach

Ingredients:

- 1 cup of mixed berries (such as strawberries, blueberries, raspberries)
- 1 cup of fresh spinach leaves
- 1 ripe banana
- 1/2 cup of Greek yogurt or coconut yogurt
- 1/2 cup of almond milk or any milk of your choice
- Optional: 1 tablespoon of honey or maple syrup for added sweetness
- Ice cubes (optional, for a colder smoothie)

Instructions:

1. Wash the mixed berries and spinach leaves thoroughly.
2. Peel the ripe banana and break it into chunks.
3. In a blender, combine the mixed berries, spinach leaves, banana chunks, Greek yogurt, and almond milk.
4. If you prefer a sweeter taste, add honey or maple syrup to the blender.
5. Optionally, add a few ice cubes if you want a colder smoothie.
6. Blend all the ingredients until smooth and creamy. If the mixture is too thick, you can add more almond milk to achieve your desired consistency.
7. Taste the smoothie and adjust sweetness if needed by adding more honey or maple syrup.
8. Once blended to your liking, pour the Super Berry Spinach smoothie into glasses and serve immediately.

This smoothie packs a punch with antioxidants, vitamins, and minerals from the berries and spinach. It's a nutritious and refreshing way to start your day or enjoy as a midday snack! Adjust the sweetness level according to your preference for a personalized touch.

Cocoa Coconut Crush

Ingredients:

- 1 ripe banana
- 2 tablespoons of cocoa powder (unsweetened)
- 1/4 cup of shredded coconut (unsweetened)
- 1 cup of coconut milk
- 1/2 cup of Greek yogurt or coconut yogurt
- Optional: 1 tablespoon of honey or maple syrup for added sweetness
- Ice cubes (optional, for a colder smoothie)

Instructions:

1. Peel the ripe banana and break it into chunks.
2. In a blender, combine the banana chunks, cocoa powder, shredded coconut, coconut milk, and Greek yogurt.
3. If you prefer a sweeter taste, add honey or maple syrup to the blender.
4. Optionally, add a few ice cubes to the blender for a colder smoothie.
5. Blend all the ingredients until smooth and creamy.
6. Taste the smoothie and adjust sweetness if needed by adding more honey or maple syrup.
7. Once blended to your liking, pour the Cocoa Coconut Crush into glasses.
8. Serve immediately and enjoy your rich and indulgent Cocoa Coconut Crush!

This smoothie combines the rich flavor of cocoa with the tropical sweetness of coconut, resulting in a creamy and satisfying treat. It's perfect for satisfying your chocolate cravings while providing a nutritious boost from the banana, yogurt, and coconut milk. Adjust the sweetness level according to your preference for a personalized experience.

Turmeric Mango Magic

Ingredients:

- 1 ripe mango, peeled and diced
- 1/2 teaspoon of ground turmeric or 1-inch piece of fresh turmeric root, peeled and grated
- 1/2 cup of Greek yogurt or coconut yogurt
- 1/2 cup of almond milk or any milk of your choice
- 1 tablespoon of honey or maple syrup (optional, for added sweetness)
- Ice cubes (optional, for a colder smoothie)

Instructions:

1. Peel and dice the ripe mango.
2. If using fresh turmeric root, peel and grate it.
3. In a blender, combine the diced mango, ground turmeric or grated fresh turmeric, Greek yogurt, almond milk, and optional honey or maple syrup.
4. Optionally, add a few ice cubes to the blender for a colder smoothie.
5. Blend all the ingredients until smooth and creamy.
6. Taste the smoothie and adjust sweetness if needed by adding more honey or maple syrup.
7. Once blended to your liking, pour the Turmeric Mango Magic into glasses.
8. Serve immediately and enjoy your refreshing and nutritious Turmeric Mango Magic smoothie!

This smoothie is not only delicious but also packed with vitamins, minerals, and antioxidants from the mango and turmeric. It's a great way to boost your immune system and promote overall well-being. Adjust the sweetness level according to your preference for a personalized experience.

Avocado Almond Dream

Ingredients:

- 1 ripe avocado, peeled and pitted
- 1 tablespoon of almond butter
- 1 cup of almond milk or any milk of your choice
- 1 tablespoon of honey or maple syrup (optional, for added sweetness)
- Ice cubes (optional, for a colder smoothie)

Instructions:

1. Scoop the flesh of the ripe avocado into a blender.
2. Add almond butter, almond milk, and optional honey or maple syrup to the blender.
3. Optionally, add a few ice cubes to the blender for a colder smoothie.
4. Blend all the ingredients until smooth and creamy.
5. Taste the smoothie and adjust sweetness if needed by adding more honey or maple syrup.
6. Once blended to your liking, pour the Avocado Almond Dream into glasses.
7. Serve immediately and enjoy your creamy and nutritious Avocado Almond Dream smoothie!

This smoothie is rich in healthy fats from the avocado and almond butter, making it a satisfying and filling drink. It's perfect for breakfast or as a snack to keep you energized throughout the day. Adjust the sweetness level according to your preference for a personalized experience.

Blueberry Basil Bliss

Ingredients:

- 1 cup of blueberries (fresh or frozen)
- 5-6 fresh basil leaves
- 1/2 cup of Greek yogurt or coconut yogurt
- 1/2 cup of almond milk or any milk of your choice
- 1 tablespoon of honey or maple syrup (optional, for added sweetness)
- Ice cubes (optional, for a colder smoothie)

Instructions:

1. Wash the blueberries and basil leaves thoroughly.
2. In a blender, combine the blueberries, basil leaves, Greek yogurt, almond milk, and optional honey or maple syrup.
3. Optionally, add a few ice cubes to the blender for a colder smoothie.
4. Blend all the ingredients until smooth and creamy.
5. Taste the smoothie and adjust sweetness if needed by adding more honey or maple syrup.
6. Once blended to your liking, pour the Blueberry Basil Bliss into glasses.
7. Serve immediately and enjoy your refreshing and flavorful Blueberry Basil Bliss smoothie!

This smoothie offers a delightful combination of sweet blueberries and aromatic basil, creating a unique and delicious flavor profile. It's packed with antioxidants, vitamins, and minerals, making it a nutritious and refreshing drink. Adjust the sweetness level according to your preference for a personalized experience.

Raspberry Coconut Refresher

Ingredients:

- 1 cup of raspberries (fresh or frozen)
- 1/2 cup of coconut milk
- 1/2 cup of Greek yogurt or coconut yogurt
- 1 tablespoon of honey or maple syrup (optional, for added sweetness)
- Juice of 1/2 lime
- Ice cubes (optional, for a colder drink)
- Fresh mint leaves for garnish (optional)

Instructions:

1. Wash the raspberries thoroughly if using fresh ones.
2. In a blender, combine the raspberries, coconut milk, Greek yogurt, lime juice, and optional honey or maple syrup.
3. Optionally, add a few ice cubes to the blender for a colder drink.
4. Blend all the ingredients until smooth and creamy.
5. Taste the drink and adjust sweetness if needed by adding more honey or maple syrup.
6. Once blended to your liking, pour the Raspberry Coconut Refresher into glasses.
7. Optionally, garnish with fresh mint leaves for a burst of flavor and visual appeal.
8. Serve immediately and enjoy your tropical and refreshing Raspberry Coconut Refresher!

This drink offers a perfect balance of tartness from the raspberries and creaminess from the coconut milk and yogurt. It's packed with flavor and nutrients, making it a delightful beverage for any time of the day. Adjust the sweetness level according to your preference for a personalized experience.

Papaya Paradise

Ingredients:

- 1 ripe papaya, peeled, seeded, and chopped
- 1 banana
- 1/2 cup of Greek yogurt or coconut yogurt
- 1/2 cup of coconut water or pineapple juice
- Juice of 1 lime
- Optional: 1 tablespoon of honey or maple syrup for added sweetness
- Ice cubes (optional, for a colder smoothie)

Instructions:

1. Peel, seed, and chop the ripe papaya.
2. Peel the banana and break it into chunks.
3. In a blender, combine the chopped papaya, banana chunks, Greek yogurt, coconut water or pineapple juice, and lime juice.
4. If you prefer a sweeter taste, add honey or maple syrup to the blender.
5. Optionally, add a few ice cubes to the blender for a colder smoothie.
6. Blend all the ingredients until smooth and creamy.
7. Taste the smoothie and adjust sweetness if needed by adding more honey or maple syrup.
8. Once blended to your liking, pour the Papaya Paradise smoothie into glasses.
9. Serve immediately and enjoy your tropical and refreshing Papaya Paradise smoothie!

This smoothie is bursting with tropical flavor from the papaya and banana, complemented by the creaminess of Greek yogurt and the tanginess of lime juice. It's a perfect way to transport yourself to a tropical paradise and enjoy a refreshing and nutritious drink. Adjust the sweetness level according to your preference for a personalized experience.

Matcha Mint Marvel

Ingredients:

- 1 teaspoon of matcha powder
- 1 cup of almond milk or any milk of your choice
- 1 handful of fresh mint leaves
- 1 tablespoon of honey or maple syrup (optional, for added sweetness)
- Ice cubes

Instructions:

1. In a small bowl, whisk the matcha powder with a small amount of hot water to create a smooth paste.
2. In a blender, combine the matcha paste, almond milk, fresh mint leaves, and optional honey or maple syrup.
3. Add ice cubes to the blender for a colder drink.
4. Blend all the ingredients until the mint leaves are finely chopped and the mixture is smooth.
5. Taste the drink and adjust sweetness if needed by adding more honey or maple syrup.
6. Once blended to your liking, pour the Matcha Mint Marvel into glasses.
7. Optionally, garnish with a sprig of fresh mint for a pop of color and flavor.
8. Serve immediately and enjoy your refreshing and invigorating Matcha Mint Marvel!

This drink combines the earthy flavor of matcha with the refreshing taste of mint, creating a harmonious and revitalizing beverage. It's perfect for a morning pick-me-up or an afternoon treat. Adjust the sweetness level according to your preference for a personalized experience.

Chocolate Cherry Bomb

Ingredients:

- 1 cup of frozen cherries (pitted)
- 1 tablespoon of cocoa powder (unsweetened)
- 1 cup of almond milk or any milk of your choice
- 1/2 cup of Greek yogurt or coconut yogurt
- 1 tablespoon of honey or maple syrup (optional, for added sweetness)
- Ice cubes (optional, for a colder smoothie)

Instructions:

1. Place the frozen cherries, cocoa powder, almond milk, Greek yogurt, and optional honey or maple syrup into a blender.
2. If you prefer a colder smoothie, add a few ice cubes to the blender.
3. Blend all the ingredients until smooth and creamy.
4. Taste the smoothie and adjust sweetness if needed by adding more honey or maple syrup.
5. Once blended to your liking, pour the Chocolate Cherry Bomb smoothie into glasses.
6. Serve immediately and enjoy your indulgent and fruity Chocolate Cherry Bomb!

This smoothie combines the rich flavors of chocolate and cherries, creating a deliciously satisfying treat. It's perfect for satisfying your sweet tooth while providing a boost of energy and nutrients. Adjust the sweetness level according to your preference for a personalized experience.

Green Goodness Galore

Ingredients:

- 1 cup of spinach leaves
- 1/2 cup of kale leaves (stems removed)
- 1/2 ripe avocado, peeled and pitted
- 1/2 cup of cucumber, chopped
- 1/2 cup of pineapple chunks (fresh or frozen)
- 1/2 banana
- 1 tablespoon of chia seeds
- 1 cup of coconut water or water
- Optional: Juice of 1/2 lime or lemon for extra freshness
- Optional: 1 tablespoon of honey or maple syrup for added sweetness
- Ice cubes (optional, for a colder smoothie)

Instructions:

1. Wash the spinach and kale leaves thoroughly.
2. In a blender, combine the spinach leaves, kale leaves, avocado, cucumber, pineapple chunks, banana, chia seeds, and coconut water or water.
3. Optionally, add the juice of half a lime or lemon for extra freshness.
4. If you prefer a sweeter taste, add honey or maple syrup to the blender.
5. Optionally, add a few ice cubes to the blender for a colder smoothie.
6. Blend all the ingredients until smooth and creamy.
7. Taste the smoothie and adjust sweetness if needed by adding more honey or maple syrup.
8. Once blended to your liking, pour the Green Goodness Galore smoothie into glasses.
9. Serve immediately and enjoy your nutritious and refreshing Green Goodness Galore smoothie!

This smoothie is packed with leafy greens, fruits, and chia seeds, providing a plethora of vitamins, minerals, fiber, and antioxidants. It's a fantastic way to start your day or replenish your body after a workout. Adjust the sweetness and tartness levels according to your preference for a personalized experience.

Goldenberry Glow

Ingredients:

- 1 cup of goldenberries (fresh or frozen)
- 1 ripe banana
- 1/2 cup of Greek yogurt or coconut yogurt
- 1/2 cup of almond milk or any milk of your choice
- 1 tablespoon of honey or maple syrup (optional, for added sweetness)
- 1 tablespoon of chia seeds
- Juice of 1/2 lemon
- Ice cubes (optional, for a colder smoothie)

Instructions:

1. Rinse the goldenberries thoroughly if using fresh ones.
2. Peel the ripe banana and break it into chunks.
3. In a blender, combine the goldenberries, banana chunks, Greek yogurt, almond milk, honey or maple syrup (if using), chia seeds, and lemon juice.
4. Optionally, add a few ice cubes to the blender for a colder smoothie.
5. Blend all the ingredients until smooth and creamy.
6. Taste the smoothie and adjust sweetness if needed by adding more honey or maple syrup.
7. Once blended to your liking, pour the Goldenberry Glow smoothie into glasses.
8. Serve immediately and enjoy your refreshing and nutrient-packed Goldenberry Glow!

This smoothie is bursting with the tangy sweetness of goldenberries, complemented by the creaminess of banana and yogurt. It's packed with vitamins, minerals, fiber, and antioxidants, making it a fantastic choice for a healthy breakfast or snack. Adjust the sweetness level according to your preference for a personalized experience.

Peachy Protein Powerhouse

Ingredients:

- 1 ripe peach, pitted and chopped
- 1/2 cup of plain Greek yogurt or coconut yogurt
- 1/2 cup of almond milk or any milk of your choice
- 1 scoop of vanilla protein powder
- 1 tablespoon of almond butter or peanut butter
- 1 tablespoon of honey or maple syrup (optional, for added sweetness)
- Ice cubes (optional, for a colder smoothie)

Instructions:

1. In a blender, combine the chopped peach, Greek yogurt, almond milk, protein powder, almond butter or peanut butter, and optional honey or maple syrup.
2. Optionally, add a few ice cubes to the blender for a colder smoothie.
3. Blend all the ingredients until smooth and creamy.
4. Taste the smoothie and adjust sweetness if needed by adding more honey or maple syrup.
5. Once blended to your liking, pour the Peachy Protein Powerhouse smoothie into glasses.
6. Serve immediately and enjoy your nutritious and satisfying Peachy Protein Powerhouse!

This smoothie is packed with protein, vitamins, and minerals from the Greek yogurt, protein powder, and nut butter. The peach adds natural sweetness and a refreshing flavor, making it a perfect post-workout recovery drink or a healthy breakfast option. Adjust the sweetness level according to your preference for a personalized experience.